Garden of Lost Socks

Written by Esi Edugyan

Illustrated by Amélie Dubois

HarperCollinsPublishersLtd

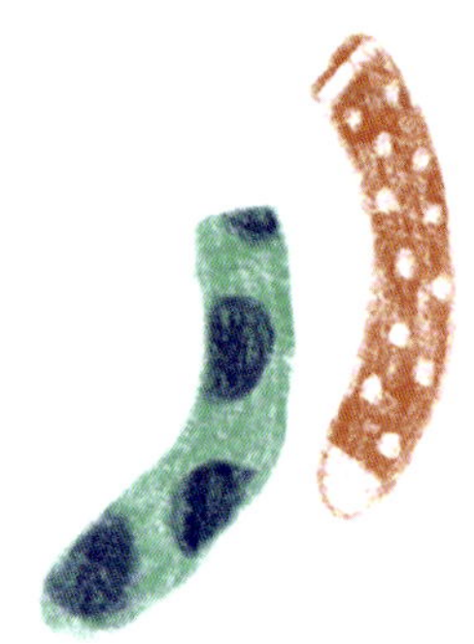

Garden of Lost Socks

Published by HarperCollins Publishers Ltd

First edition

HarperCollins books may be purchased for educational, business or sales promotional use through our Special Markets Department.

HarperCollins Publishers Ltd
Bay Adelaide Centre, East Tower
22 Adelaide Street West, 41st Floor
Toronto, Ontario, Canada
M5H 4E3

www.harpercollins.ca

Library and Archives Canada Cataloguing in Publication
Title: Garden of lost socks / Esi Edugyan ; illustrated by Amélie Dubois.
Names: Edugyan, Esi, author. | Dubois, Amélie, 1979- illustrator.
Identifiers: Canadiana (print) 20230158l8 | Canadiana (ebook) 20230l5826
ISBN 9781443464734 (hardcover) | ISBN 9781443464741 (EPUB)
Classification: LCC PS8559.D795 G37 2023 | DDC jC813/.6—dc23

Printed and bound in Italy
RTL 10 9 8 7 6 5 4 3 2 1

For Cleo and Maddox —E.E.

To my precious Dahlia —A.D.

Akosua was always told she was too nosey.

Her parents loved her very much,
but she always seemed to find trouble.

"I'm an exquirologist," said Akosua.
"I can find anything!"

“Except for friends,” said her brothers, laughing at her.

Outside, she found a boy sitting on the front stoop of his building, writing in a notebook. "What are you writing about?" asked Akosua.

“My right sock is missing!” said the boy, whose name was Max.

“Why don’t you just wear a different pair?”

“They’re my favourite,” said Max. “They are yellow, green and red with black stars on them. My nana basia sent them all the way from Ghana.”

“I can find them,” said Akosua. “I’m an exquirologist.”

“What’s that?”

“A finder of lost things.”

"I'm a journalist," said Max.

"What's that?"

"I write about things that have been found."

Max showed Akosua his notebook.

He had written many stories about their neighbourhood.

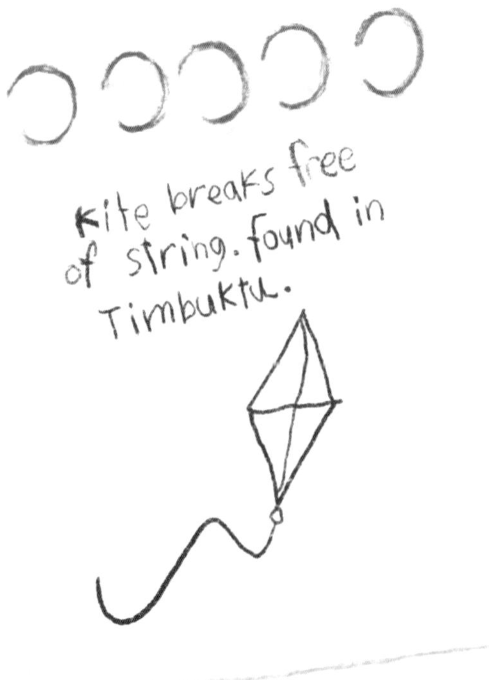

“Together we can find the sock!”

They started at Max's house, in the room he shared with his older brother. Akosua found one pair with red and green stripes, one pair with dancing kangaroos eating blue ice cream, and one pair that was black with white stars all over it.

But none were yellow, green and red with black stars on them.

They went to the laundromat on the corner.
As they searched and searched for Max's sock,
something on the folding counter caught Akosua's eye.
"Look—a longhorn beetle!" She touched it with her finger.
"It's missing a leg! That's good luck. We will for sure find your sock!"

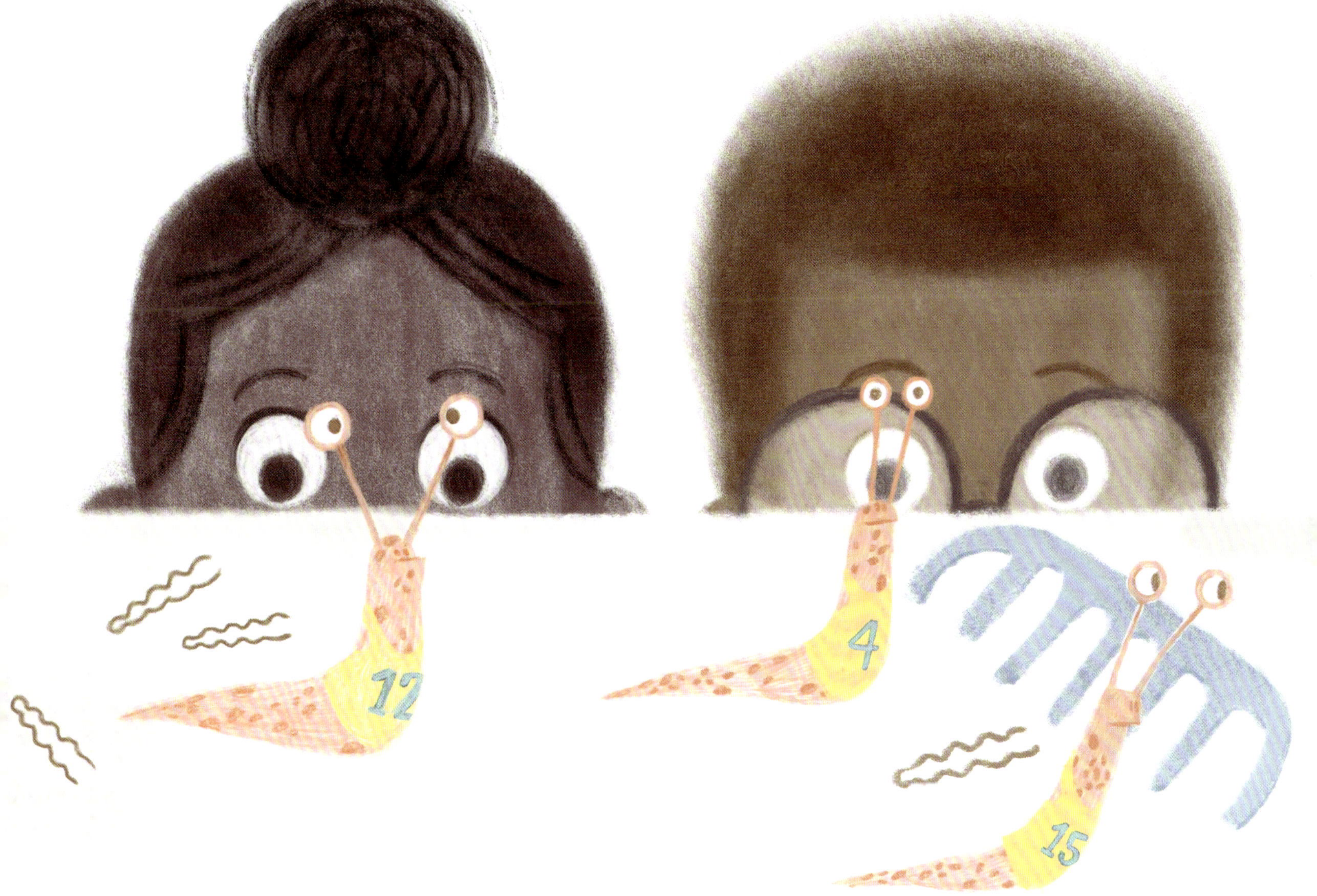

Next, they went to Yolande's barbershop and inspected every foot inside. Akosua noticed a slug race taking place. But no time to watch! They had to keep looking for the lost sock.

They passed by the open door of a house. Akosua gasped, grabbing Max's arm. The boy standing in the doorway had more than 50 feet!

"Maybe he has my sock!" said Max.

They rushed into the house. The boy stepped back in surprise.

But all his feet stayed in place.
They were only the shoes of guests
who'd come for an afternoon party.

They went to Balmoral Street, where the trees wore socks knit by the people of the neighbourhood, to keep them cozy on windy nights.

But none of the socks were yellow,
green and red with black stars.

Max's BREAKING NEWS:

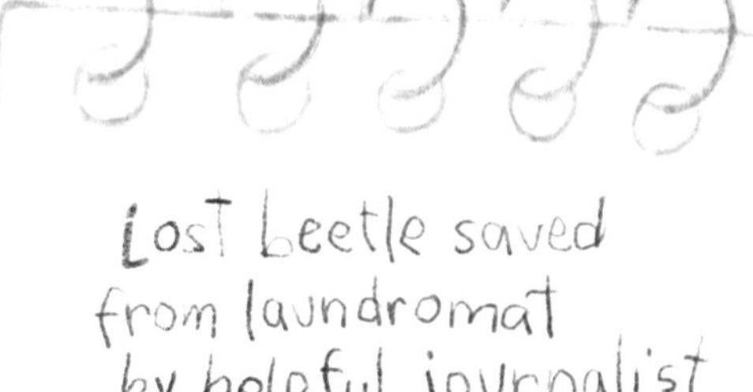

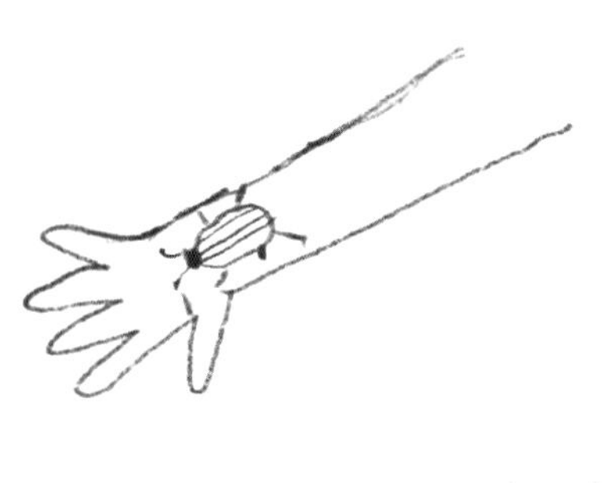

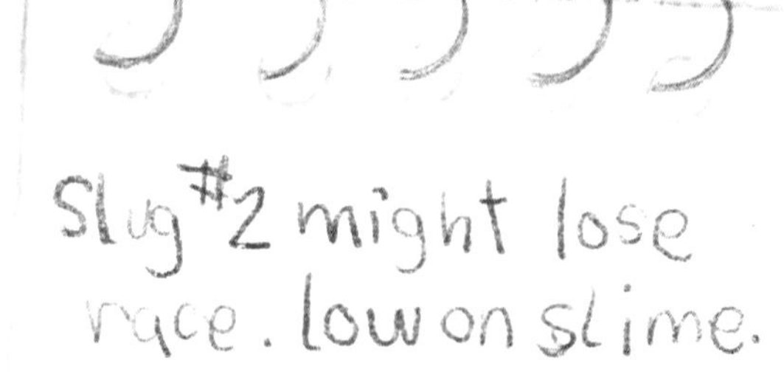

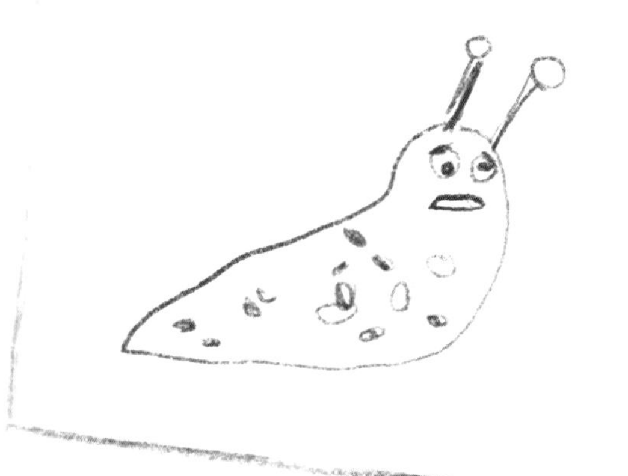

“Look!” said Akosua, pointing up at the sky.

The hot-air balloon looked like it was made of socks stitched together.

But even from the sidewalk they could see that
none were yellow, green and red with black stars.

Just then, something touched Max's leg. He jumped. It was a cat—and in her teeth was a bright pink sock!

“Let’s follow her!”

They squeezed through the gates of the community garden, where the people of the neighbourhood grew peppers and parsley and squash, and where they picked plums and pears and peaches to take home to their families. The garden almost seemed to be growing a whole patch of colourful socks, too.

“Look—there is your sock!” said Akosua.

“The cat is making a home for her kittens!”

Someone needed his sock more than Max did.
It was making their world a little warmer.

Back at Akosua's house, they wrote a news story together, to send to Max's nana basia.

Breaking news:
Missing sock finds new
life as home for 6th
kitten of peach-eating cat

They had found Max's missing sock, yes.
But there would always be something new to find.